# COMPLETE CARE FOR REPTILES AND AMPHIBIANS

## From Setting Up Habitats to Solving Common Problems

Akosua Eno

# Table of Contents

# **INTRODUCTION**

Reptiles and amphibians are fascinating groups of animals that share a variety of biological traits and evolutionary histories, yet they each possess distinct characteristics that set them apart. These creatures, often found in diverse habitats around the world, have adapted to a wide range of environmental conditions, making them unique in the animal kingdom.

Reptiles, including snakes, lizards, turtles, and crocodiles, are primarily land-dwelling creatures, though some species, such as sea turtles, thrive in aquatic environments. They are characterized by their dry, scaly skin, which helps prevent water loss in arid conditions. Reptiles are cold-blooded, meaning their body temperature fluctuates with their surroundings, and they generally lay eggs with leathery shells, although some, like certain snakes, give birth to live young.

Amphibians, such as frogs, salamanders, and newts, live in both aquatic and terrestrial environments. They have smooth, moist skin that helps them absorb oxygen and regulate moisture. Unlike reptiles, amphibians are cold-blooded but often undergo a dramatic metamorphosis, transitioning from aquatic larvae (like tadpoles) to their adult forms. Amphibians rely heavily on water for reproduction, with most species laying their eggs in aquatic environments.

Despite their differences, both reptiles and amphibians are vital components of ecosystems, playing important roles in food webs and contributing to the balance of nature. Understanding their biology, behavior, and conservation needs is crucial for appreciating the complexity of life on Earth and ensuring their survival in a changing world.

# UNDERSTANDING THE DIFFERENCE BETWEEN REPTILES AND AMPHIBIANS

Reptiles and amphibians are both fascinating groups of animals, but they have distinct biological characteristics that set them apart. While they share some similarities, such as being cold-blooded (ectothermic), their differences are key in understanding their unique adaptations and life cycles.

1. Habitat and Lifestyle:

• Reptiles: These animals are predominantly land-dwellers, although some species, like sea turtles, live in water. Reptiles are well-suited for terrestrial environments due to their adaptations, such as dry, scaly skin that prevents water loss. They are mostly found in warmer climates and are adapted to survive in a range of ecosystems, from deserts to forests.

- Amphibians: Amphibians, such as frogs, salamanders, and newts, are typically found in both aquatic and terrestrial environments. Many species start their lives in water as larvae and then undergo metamorphosis to become adults capable of living on land. Their moist, permeable skin allows them to absorb oxygen and moisture, but it also means they are often dependent on damp habitats to prevent dehydration.

2. Skin Type:

- Reptiles: Reptiles have dry, scaly skin that helps conserve water and protect them from harsh environmental conditions. This skin is covered in keratin, the same material that makes up human hair and nails, and it is periodically shed in a process called ecdysis.

- Amphibians: In contrast, amphibians have smooth, moist skin that facilitates gas exchange and hydration. Their skin is highly permeable, allowing them to absorb water and oxygen directly through it, which is why many amphibians are found in humid environments or near water.

3. Reproduction:

• Reptiles: Reptiles generally lay eggs with leathery shells that protect the developing embryos from drying out. Some species, like certain snakes and lizards, give birth to live young. Reptile eggs are typically laid on land, and the young are independent upon hatching.

• Amphibians: Amphibians usually lay their eggs in water, where the larvae (such as tadpoles) hatch and undergo metamorphosis into adult forms. Most amphibians do not have protective eggshells, and their eggs are vulnerable to drying out, which is why they are often found in aquatic or moist environments.

4. Temperature Regulation:

• Reptiles: As cold-blooded animals, reptiles rely on external sources of heat to regulate their body temperature. They often bask in the sun to warm up and seek shade to cool down.

• Amphibians: Amphibians are also cold-blooded but have a greater reliance on moisture for regulating body temperature. Their permeable skin makes them more sensitive to changes in their environment, which is why they are often found in places where humidity is high.

5. Life Cycle:

• Reptiles: Reptiles generally have a straightforward life cycle. They lay eggs, and the young usually hatch in a form that closely resembles adults, though they may undergo growth stages, such as a juvenile stage.

• Amphibians: Amphibians undergo a more complex life cycle, involving metamorphosis. This starts with an aquatic larval stage (like tadpoles in frogs) that gradually changes into a terrestrial adult form with legs and lungs for land-based living. While reptiles and amphibians share some similarities as ectothermic animals, their differences in habitat, skin structure, reproduction, and life cycle illustrate the distinct evolutionary paths they have taken. Reptiles are better adapted for land-based life with their scaly skin and leathery eggs, whereas amphibians have evolved to thrive in both aquatic and terrestrial environments, relying on moisture and undergoing metamorphosis. Understanding these differences helps us appreciate the diverse ways in which these animals have adapted to their surroundings and continue to thrive in ecosystems around the world.

# WHY KEEP REPTILES AND AMPHIBIANS AS PETS

Reptiles and amphibians can make fascinating and rewarding pets, offering a unique experience for animal lovers. Whether you're drawn to their low-maintenance care, distinctive behaviors, or the opportunity to observe their natural instincts up close, there are several reasons why people choose to keep these creatures as pets. Here are some of the top reasons:

1. Low Maintenance

Reptiles and amphibians are generally low-maintenance compared to more traditional pets like dogs or cats. They don't require daily walks, grooming, or constant attention. Many species, such as turtles, geckos, or frogs, can thrive in a controlled habitat with minimal intervention, making them ideal for individuals or families with busy lifestyles.

2. Unique and Fascinating Behaviors

Reptiles and amphibians exhibit behaviors that are incredibly interesting to watch. From the way a snake sheds its skin to a frog's jumping abilities, these animals offer a glimpse into nature's diversity. Their behaviors can be both calming and captivating, providing a sense of connection to wildlife. For example, many reptile species have unique feeding habits, and amphibians often display intricate courtship rituals during mating season.

3. Educational Value

Keeping reptiles and amphibians as pets provides an excellent opportunity to learn about animal biology, evolution, and ecosystems. These creatures offer insights into how different species adapt to their environments. Observing the life cycle of amphibians, such as tadpoles transforming into adult frogs, or studying the thermoregulation behaviors of reptiles, can be an engaging educational experience, especially for children.

4. Space-Efficient Pets

Reptiles and amphibians are often a great choice for people with limited living space. Unlike large mammals that require substantial space to roam, many reptiles (like geckos, snakes, and turtles) can live comfortably in small enclosures such as aquariums or terrariums. Their compact size and controlled care requirements make them suitable for apartments or homes without yards.

5. Allergy-Free Companions

For people who suffer from allergies to pet dander, reptiles and amphibians can be a welcome alternative. These animals don't shed fur or produce dander, making them ideal for allergy sufferers. As a result, many individuals who can't keep traditional pets due to allergies find reptiles and amphibians to be a safe and enjoyable option.

## 6. A Wide Variety of Species

There is an incredible variety of reptile and amphibian species to choose from, each with its own distinct characteristics and care needs. Whether you're interested in a colorful frog, a docile turtle, or an exotic snake, there's something for every pet owner. This variety allows enthusiasts to choose an animal that fits their lifestyle, from easy-to-care-for species like leopard geckos to more exotic pets like chameleons or iguanas.

## 7. Long Lifespan

Many reptiles, such as turtles, can live for decades, and some species of snakes or lizards can live 15–20 years or longer. This longevity makes reptiles and amphibians a long-term companion for those prepared to care for them. For individuals seeking a lasting pet, reptiles and amphibians can form an enduring bond with their owners.

8. Low-Cost Care

Although the initial setup for reptiles and amphibians can be a bit of an investment—particularly for specialized tanks, lighting, and heating systems—ongoing care tends to be affordable. Unlike feeding mammals, reptiles and amphibians typically have simpler dietary needs, often consuming insects, vegetables, or pre-packaged reptile food. Their housing setup requires regular cleaning, but they don't typically need expensive grooming or regular vet visits.

9. Conservation Efforts

By keeping reptiles and amphibians as pets, people can help raise awareness about species that may be endangered or threatened in the wild. Many responsible pet owners buy their reptiles from breeders who follow ethical practices, which helps prevent the overharvesting of wild populations. In some cases, pet owners also support conservation initiatives or participate in breeding programs to preserve rare or endangered species.

10. Stress Reduction and Therapeutic Benefits

Interacting with reptiles and amphibians can have a calming, therapeutic effect. Watching a reptile bask in the sun or a frog hop across a tank can be a peaceful and soothing experience. Reptiles, in particular, are often less demanding than other pets and can help reduce stress through their quiet, serene presence. For some pet owners, simply observing these animals in their habitat offers relaxation and a connection to nature. Reptiles and amphibians offer a unique and rewarding pet experience. They require less maintenance, provide educational and fascinating insights into nature, and can be suitable for people with allergies or limited space. With their diverse behaviors, long lifespans, and ability to thrive in relatively simple setups, they can be the perfect companions for those seeking something different from the traditional pet experience. Whether you're an experienced enthusiast or a beginner, reptiles and amphibians can offer both joy and a deeper understanding of the natural world.

# CHAPTER ONE

## THE FASCINATING WORLD OF COLD-BLOODED CREATURES

Cold-blooded creatures, also known as ectotherms, are some of the most intriguing animals on Earth. These fascinating beings, which include reptiles, amphibians, fish, and even some invertebrates, have evolved unique ways of surviving and thriving in a world where temperature regulation is a constant challenge. Unlike warm-blooded creatures (endotherms), whose bodies can maintain a constant internal temperature, cold-blooded animals rely on external sources of heat to regulate their body temperature. This distinction not only affects their biology but also influences their behavior, habitat choices, and overall lifestyle.

1. What Does It Mean to Be Cold-Blooded?

Cold-bloodedness refers to an animal's inability to regulate its body temperature internally. Instead, the body temperature of cold-blooded creatures fluctuates with the surrounding environment. If the weather is warm, their body temperature rises; if it's cold, their body temperature drops. This characteristic makes these animals particularly dependent on external factors such as sunlight, water temperature, and the warmth of their surroundings.

2. How Cold-Blooded Creatures Adapt to Their Environments

Cold-blooded creatures have developed a variety of strategies to cope with temperature changes in their environments. Some of these strategies include:

• Basking: Many reptiles, such as lizards and snakes, rely on basking in the sun to absorb heat and raise their body temperature. This behavior helps them maintain the energy needed for digestion, movement, and survival. After basking, they often retreat to the shade to avoid overheating.

• Hibernation or Brumation: During colder months, many cold-blooded animals enter a state of dormancy to conserve energy. Amphibians, such as frogs, may hibernate in the mud at the bottom of ponds, while reptiles like snakes may brumate in burrows or underground spaces where the temperature remains more stable.

• Nocturnal Activity: Some cold-blooded creatures, like certain reptiles and amphibians, are nocturnal, becoming more active during the cooler evening hours to avoid the heat of the day. This helps them maintain a more comfortable body temperature while still finding food and shelter.

### 3. The Role of Cold-Blooded Creatures in Ecosystems

Cold-blooded animals play crucial roles in ecosystems. As predators, they help control populations of smaller creatures, such as insects, rodents, and amphibians. As prey, they provide a food source for larger animals, creating a balanced food web. In aquatic ecosystems, fish and amphibians are essential for maintaining healthy water systems, as they often help regulate the populations of insects and other invertebrates.

These animals are also vital in nutrient cycling. For example, many amphibians help fertilize soil by decomposing plant material and consuming a wide range of insects, while reptiles like turtles and crocodiles contribute to maintaining the balance of wetland ecosystems.

4. Unique Features of Cold-Blooded Creatures

Cold-blooded creatures are incredibly diverse, and their adaptability is reflected in their unique features:

• Scaly Skin of Reptiles: Reptiles such as snakes, turtles, and lizards have developed tough, scaly skin to protect them from dehydration, predation, and environmental stress. Unlike mammals, reptiles do not lose water through sweat, which allows them to survive in dry or arid environments.

• Metamorphosis in Amphibians: Amphibians such as frogs and salamanders go through a dramatic metamorphosis from aquatic larvae (like tadpoles) to their adult form, which may be adapted to life on land. This ability to transition between two distinct environments showcases their incredible versatility.

• Specialized Respiratory Systems: Many cold-blooded creatures have evolved specialized respiratory systems. For example, amphibians rely on both their lungs and skin for respiration, absorbing oxygen through their moist skin. Some reptiles, such as certain species of turtles, can also absorb oxygen through their skin, allowing them to remain submerged for extended periods.

5. The Diversity of Cold-Blooded Creatures

The world of cold-blooded creatures is incredibly diverse, with species occupying nearly every corner of the globe. Some notable groups include:

• Reptiles: Snakes, lizards, turtles, and crocodiles are well-known examples of reptiles. These animals can be found in a variety of habitats, from deserts to tropical rainforests to oceans.

• Amphibians: Frogs, toads, salamanders, and newts make up the amphibian group. These creatures typically spend part of their lives in water and part on land, undergoing significant transformations in their life cycle.

• Fish: Cold-blooded fish such as sharks, trout, and goldfish are crucial in aquatic ecosystems. They have evolved unique adaptations for swimming and breathing underwater, and they come in a vast range of sizes and shapes.

• Invertebrates: Some invertebrates, like certain species of insects, spiders, and crustaceans, are also ectothermic. These creatures are often more active in warmer temperatures and play important roles in pollination, decomposition, and as a food source for other animals.

6. The Challenges of Cold-Bloodedness

While cold-blooded creatures have many adaptations that help them survive in fluctuating temperatures, they face challenges that warm-blooded animals do not. For instance, their metabolic rate is closely tied to the environment, meaning they may struggle to find food or maintain energy levels during extreme temperature fluctuations. In colder climates, these creatures may face difficulties during winter, while in hotter climates, they may overheat if they cannot find shade or water.

7. Conservation of Cold-Blooded Creatures

Many cold-blooded species are facing threats due to habitat loss, climate change, pollution, and overhunting. Amphibians, in particular, are highly sensitive to environmental changes and are often the first to show signs of ecosystem distress. Conservation efforts are crucial to protect these animals, including habitat restoration, breeding programs, and policies to reduce human impact on natural habitats. The world of cold-blooded creatures is rich with diversity and complexity. These animals have evolved extraordinary adaptations to thrive in environments where others may not survive. From basking in the sun to undergoing metamorphosis, cold-blooded creatures offer endless opportunities for study and fascination. Their roles in ecosystems are invaluable, and protecting them ensures that the delicate balance of our natural world remains intact. Understanding and appreciating these remarkable animals helps us not only protect them but also gain a deeper respect for the resilience of life on Earth.

## OVERVIEW OF POPULAR SPECIES OF COLD-BLOODED CREATURES

Cold-blooded animals are some of the most diverse and fascinating creatures on Earth. From reptiles and amphibians to fish and invertebrates, these species display a remarkable range of adaptations and behaviors suited to their environments. Below is an overview of some of the most popular species across these groups, showcasing their unique characteristics, habitats, and appeal as pets or subjects of study.

1. Reptiles

Reptiles are among the most well-known cold-blooded creatures. They are characterized by their scaly skin, internal fertilization, and ability to lay eggs with leathery shells (though some species give birth to live young). Here are some popular reptilian species:

• Green Iguana (Iguana iguana)

Habitat: Rainforests and tropical regions of Central and South America.

Size: Up to 6 feet in length.

Diet: Herbivorous, primarily feeding on leaves, flowers, and fruit.

Popularity as Pets: Known for their docile nature, but they require large enclosures and a warm environment.

Interesting Fact: Green iguanas can swim and are excellent climbers.

• Leopard Gecko (Eublepharis macularius)

Habitat: Native to the arid regions of Afghanistan, Pakistan, and India.

Size: Around 8–10 inches in length.

Diet: Insectivorous, feeding on crickets, mealworms, and other insects.

Popularity as Pets: One of the most popular pet reptiles due to their small size, gentle temperament, and ease of care.

Interesting Fact: Leopard geckos have a unique ability to regenerate their tails if lost.

• Ball Python (Python regius)

Habitat: Sub-Saharan Africa, typically in grasslands and forests.

Size: Typically 3–5 feet in length.

Diet: Carnivorous, primarily feeding on rodents and birds.

Popularity as Pets: Popular for their calm temperament and relatively manageable size.

Interesting Fact: Ball pythons are known for curling into a ball when threatened, hence their name.

• Bearded Dragon (Pogona vitticeps)

Habitat: Native to the deserts of Australia.

Size: Can grow up to 24 inches in length.

Diet: Omnivorous, feeding on insects, fruits, and vegetables.

Popularity as Pets: Known for their friendly disposition and ease of care.

Interesting Fact: Bearded dragons can puff out the skin around their neck to appear larger when threatened.

2. Amphibians

Amphibians are cold-blooded vertebrates that live part of their lives in water and part on land. They are characterized by their moist, permeable skin and typically undergo metamorphosis during their life cycle. Some popular amphibian species include:

• American Bullfrog (Rana catesbeiana)

Habitat: Ponds, lakes, and wetlands in North America.

Size: Can grow up to 8 inches in length.

Diet: Carnivorous, feeding on insects, small fish, and even small mammals.

Popularity as Pets: Often kept in ponds or aquariums for their distinctive croaking sound and large size.

Interesting Fact: Bullfrogs are known for their powerful jump and are capable of leaping up to 10 times their body length.

• Axolotl (Ambystoma mexicanum)

Habitat: Native to lakes in Mexico, particularly Lake Xochimilco.

Size: Typically 6–12 inches long.

Diet: Carnivorous, eating worms, small fish, and larvae.

Popularity as Pets: Known for their regenerative abilities, the axolotl is a popular exotic pet.

Interesting Fact: Axolotls retain their larval form throughout life (a condition known as neoteny) and can regenerate lost limbs, spinal cord, and even parts of their heart.

• Fire-Bellied Toad (Bombina orientalis)

Habitat: Native to East Asia, particularly in China and Korea.

Size: Up to 2 inches in length.

Diet: Insectivorous, eating small invertebrates such as crickets.

Popularity as Pets: Popular for their striking appearance and vibrant red or orange belly.

Interesting Fact: When threatened, fire-bellied toads flip onto their backs to reveal their brightly colored underside, which serves as a warning to predators.

3. Fish

Fish are one of the most diverse groups of cold-blooded animals, occupying environments from deep oceans to freshwater lakes and rivers. Some popular fish species include:

• Betta Fish (Betta splendens)

Habitat: Native to Southeast Asia, especially in Thailand and Cambodia.

Size: Typically 2–3 inches in length.

Diet: Carnivorous, feeding on small insects and larvae.

Popularity as Pets: Known for their vivid colors and long, flowing fins. They are often kept in small tanks.

Interesting Fact: Male bettas are known for their aggressive territorial behavior and will fight other males.

• Goldfish (Carassius auratus)

Habitat: Native to East Asia, commonly found in ponds and aquariums.

Size: Varies, but typically 6–8 inches in length (can grow much larger in the wild).

Diet: Omnivorous, eating both plant matter and small aquatic animals.

Popularity as Pets: One of the most popular pet fish due to their easy care and variety of colors.

Interesting Fact: Goldfish have an impressive memory and can recognize their owners.

• Clownfish (Amphiprioninae)

Habitat: Found in the warm, shallow waters of the Pacific and Indian Oceans.

Size: Typically 3–4 inches in length.

Diet: Omnivorous, feeding on zooplankton and algae.

Popularity as Pets: Famous for their symbiotic relationship with sea anemones and popularized by the movie Finding Nemo.

Interesting Fact: Clownfish are immune to the stings of sea anemones, thanks to a special mucus on their skin.

4. Invertebrates

Invertebrates, such as certain species of insects, arachnids, and crustaceans, are also cold-blooded and can be fascinating to keep as pets. Some popular invertebrates include:

• Tarantula (Theraphosidae family)

Habitat: Native to tropical regions of Central and South America, Asia, and Africa.

Size: Varies by species, but can range from 4 to 12 inches in leg span.

Diet: Carnivorous, primarily feeding on insects and small vertebrates.

Popularity as Pets: Popular among exotic pet enthusiasts due to their impressive size and striking appearance.

Interesting Fact: Tarantulas can live for up to 30 years in captivity, and they molt their exoskeleton several times throughout their life.

• Hermit Crab (Coenobita species)

Habitat: Found in coastal regions, often in the Caribbean or Pacific islands.

Size: Typically 2–3 inches in length.

Diet: Omnivorous, feeding on detritus, fruit, and small animals.

Popularity as Pets: Popular for their low-maintenance care and amusing behavior.

Interesting Fact: Hermit crabs use empty shells to protect their soft bodies and will switch shells as they grow.

Cold-blooded creatures are as varied as they are fascinating, with each species offering unique traits and behaviors. Whether it's the majestic bearded dragon basking in the sun, the axolotl's incredible regenerative abilities, or the colorful goldfish swimming gracefully in a tank, these animals continue to captivate enthusiasts and researchers alike. Their adaptability and diversity make them an essential part of the natural world, and their popularity as pets highlights the deep connection humans have with these remarkable creatures.

## THE BASICS OF REPTILE AND AMPHIBIAN BIOLOGY

Reptiles and amphibians are two distinct groups of cold-blooded vertebrates that share some similarities but also exhibit a wide range of differences in their biology and life processes. Understanding their anatomy, physiology, metabolism, and life cycle offers insight into their adaptability and unique roles in ecosystems. Below is an overview of these key aspects of reptile and amphibian biology.

# ANATOMY AND PHYSIOLOGY OF REPTILES

Reptiles, which include snakes, lizards, turtles, and crocodiles, have evolved to thrive in a variety of environments, from deserts to rainforests. Their anatomy and physiology are well-suited to land-based life, with several key features:

• Skin: Reptiles have dry, scaly skin made of keratin, which helps prevent water loss. The skin sheds periodically in a process known as ecdysis.

• Skeleton: Reptiles have a well-developed internal skeleton, with a strong vertebral column. Most reptiles have a bony ribcage, unlike amphibians.

• Respiration: Reptiles breathe using lungs. They rely on diaphragm-like muscles to assist in breathing, a more efficient system than the simple diffusion used by amphibians.

• Circulatory System: Reptiles typically have a three-chambered heart (except for crocodiles, which have a four-chambered heart), and they circulate oxygenated and deoxygenated blood through different parts of the body. This allows for more effective oxygenation of tissues compared to amphibians.

• Temperature Regulation: Being ectothermic (cold-blooded), reptiles regulate their body temperature through external means such as basking in the sun or seeking shade.

## ANATOMY AND PHYSIOLOGY OF AMPHIBIANS

Amphibians, which include frogs, salamanders, newts, and caecilians, have adapted to both aquatic and terrestrial environments during their life stages. Their anatomy and physiology are more suited to environments with significant moisture.

• Skin: Amphibians have thin, permeable skin that allows for the absorption of oxygen and water directly through the skin. This characteristic makes them highly sensitive to environmental changes, particularly pollution. Some amphibians secrete toxins through their skin as a defense mechanism.

• Skeleton: Amphibians have a less robust skeleton compared to reptiles. Their bones are lighter, allowing for better movement in water and on land. Many amphibians have strong, muscular limbs for jumping or swimming.

• Respiration: Amphibians often rely on both their lungs and skin for respiration. During the larval stage, most amphibians breathe through gills, and as adults, they develop lungs but may continue to absorb oxygen through their skin.

• Circulatory System: Amphibians have a three-chambered heart, similar to reptiles, but their circulatory system is less efficient in separating oxygenated and deoxygenated blood. This system is suitable for their dual life in water and on land.

• Temperature Regulation: Amphibians are ectothermic like reptiles, but they are more sensitive to temperature fluctuations. They rely heavily on their surroundings to regulate body temperature, such as hiding in cool, damp places during hot weather.

## METABOLISM AND ENVIRONMENTAL ADAPTATION

Both reptiles and amphibians are ectothermic, meaning their body temperature is regulated by the environment, rather than internally as in warm-blooded animals. This has significant implications for their metabolism and adaptation to various habitats.

• Metabolism in Reptiles: Reptiles generally have a slower metabolism compared to warm-blooded animals. Their metabolism is more energy-efficient, as they do not need to maintain a constant body temperature. This adaptation allows them to survive in environments where food may be scarce, as they can go for longer periods without eating. However, their metabolic rate increases with external temperature, so they are more active in warmer conditions.

• Metabolism in Amphibians: Amphibians also have a slower metabolic rate compared to warm-blooded animals, and their metabolism is highly influenced by temperature and moisture. In cooler temperatures, amphibians become less active, and some may enter a state of dormancy or hibernation to conserve energy. Additionally, their metabolic rates may decrease during periods of dryness, as they rely on moisture for respiration and hydration.

- Adaptation to Environment: Reptiles and amphibians have evolved various mechanisms to adapt to their environment. For example, many reptiles have specialized scales that reduce water loss in arid environments, while amphibians have moist skin that aids in respiration and hydration, essential in wet habitats. Some amphibians, such as the wood frog, are capable of surviving freezing temperatures by entering a state of dormancy, while reptiles, like desert tortoises, have adapted to extreme heat by burrowing or being active during cooler times of the day.

## THE LIFE CYCLE FROM EGG TO ADULT

The life cycle of reptiles and amphibians involves dramatic changes from the egg or larval stage to the adult form, but the process varies significantly between the two groups.

## Reptile Life Cycle

• Egg Stage: Most reptiles lay eggs with leathery shells (though some give birth to live young), and the embryos inside the eggs develop in a relatively protected environment. The eggs are typically laid in safe, warm places to ensure proper incubation.

• Hatchling Stage: Once the eggs hatch, the young reptiles are fully formed, although they may be smaller and less developed than the adult form. Some reptiles, like snakes and lizards, may receive little to no parental care after birth.

• Juvenile Stage: Reptiles grow steadily throughout their juvenile stage, gradually reaching sexual maturity. Many species of reptiles, such as turtles and crocodiles, may have a prolonged juvenile stage, growing slowly over many years.

• Adult Stage: Reptiles reach full maturity and are capable of reproducing. Some species may continue growing throughout their lives, especially those with indeterminate growth, like crocodiles.

## Amphibian Life Cycle

• Egg Stage: Amphibians generally lay their eggs in water, where they develop into larvae. Amphibian eggs are often coated in a gelatinous substance to protect them from desiccation. The eggs hatch into aquatic larvae (tadpoles or larvae in the case of salamanders and newts).

• Larval Stage: The larvae breathe through gills and feed on aquatic plants or small invertebrates. This stage varies in length depending on the species and environmental conditions. During this time, the amphibians undergo significant physiological changes.

• Metamorphosis: Amphibians undergo a dramatic metamorphosis, where they transition from larvae to adult form. This may involve the development of limbs, lungs, and the reabsorption of the tail in species like frogs. Some amphibians, like salamanders, may retain their larval features in adulthood (neoteny).

• Adult Stage: After metamorphosis, the adult amphibian can typically live on land or in water, depending on the species. Adult amphibians may return to water to reproduce, completing their life cycle.

Understanding the anatomy, physiology, metabolism, and life cycle of reptiles and amphibians highlights their remarkable adaptability to diverse environments. Whether they are basking in the sun to regulate their body temperature, breathing through their skin, or undergoing metamorphosis, these creatures have evolved to thrive in a variety of habitats. Their cold-blooded nature and unique life histories allow them to occupy ecological niches that warm-blooded animals cannot, making them an integral part of the animal kingdom.

# SETTING UP THE PERFECT HABITAT FOR REPTILES AND AMPHIBIANS

Creating a suitable and comfortable habitat is one of the most important aspects of keeping reptiles and amphibians as pets. These cold-blooded creatures depend on their environment to regulate their body temperature, humidity, and overall well-being. Whether you're housing a snake, a lizard, a frog, or a turtle, providing the right setup can help ensure your pet thrives. Below are essential considerations when setting up the perfect habitat for reptiles and amphibians.

# CHOOSING THE RIGHT ENCLOSURE TANK VS TERRARIUM

The first step in creating a proper habitat is selecting the right enclosure. The type of enclosure you choose depends on the species you are keeping and their natural environment. Generally, reptiles and amphibians are housed in either tanks or terrariums.

• Tank: Glass aquariums are a popular choice for reptiles and amphibians. They come in a variety of sizes and allow for easy viewing. Tanks are often best suited for aquatic or semi-aquatic species, such as turtles, frogs, or newts. They offer ample space for water and land areas if required. Tanks with lids help prevent escapes and maintain proper humidity.

• Terrarium: Terrariums are ideal for land-dwelling reptiles and amphibians, such as lizards, geckos, and terrestrial frogs. These enclosures often come with more ventilation than tanks and can help maintain a dry or humid environment, depending on the needs of the species. Terrariums are great for creating a more naturalistic environment with plants, rocks, and other decorations. When selecting your enclosure, consider the size of your pet, the type of species, and how much space they need to move around. It's important to provide enough room for your pet to engage in natural behaviors, like climbing or burrowing. Additionally, ensure the enclosure has proper ventilation to prevent mold growth and ensure air circulation.

## PROPER LIGHTING, HEATING, AND HUMIDITY

Proper lighting, heating, and humidity are crucial to replicating the natural environment of reptiles and amphibians. These factors help regulate your pet's metabolism, behavior, and overall health.

• Lighting: Most reptiles and amphibians require UVB lighting to synthesize vitamin D3, which helps them absorb calcium and maintain healthy bones. UVB lights should be on for about 10 to 12 hours a day, mimicking the natural day-night cycle. Depending on your species, you may also need to provide UVA lighting, which encourages natural activity and enhances their color.

• Heating: Reptiles, being ectothermic, rely on external heat sources to regulate their body temperature. The temperature in the enclosure should be adjustable to allow your pet to move between warmer and cooler areas. Use heat lamps, ceramic heaters, or heating pads designed for reptile habitats. The ideal temperature varies depending on the species, but it generally ranges from 75°F to 95°F (24°C to 35°C), with a basking area that's even warmer.

• Humidity: Humidity levels are particularly important for amphibians, as they rely on moisture to keep their skin hydrated and to breathe through it. Species like frogs and salamanders require high humidity levels (50% to 80%), while reptiles like desert species need lower humidity. You can control humidity using a combination of misting, water dishes, and substrates that retain moisture. A hygrometer can help you monitor the levels.

## CREATING NATURALISTIC ENVIRONMENTS FOR DIFFERENT SPECIES

Recreating a natural habitat for your reptile or amphibian can enhance their well-being and provide a more stimulating environment. The goal is to provide a space that mimics their natural surroundings, offering places for hiding, climbing, basking, or swimming.

• For Terrestrial Species: You can replicate forest floors, deserts, or grasslands, depending on the species you keep. For example, for a desert-dwelling reptile like a bearded dragon, you can use dry substrates such as sand or gravel, and provide rocks for climbing. For a rainforest species like a tree frog, you may use moist substrates like coconut fiber or sphagnum moss, along with live plants that increase humidity and provide hiding spots.

• For Aquatic Species: Aquatic reptiles and amphibians, like turtles or aquatic frogs, require both land and water areas in their enclosures. A basking spot should be included for species like turtles, along with water that is deep enough for swimming. Use water filters to keep the water clean and clear.

• For Semi-Aquatic Species: Species like the axolotl or certain frogs may need both wet and dry areas in their enclosure. Create shallow water areas with rocks or platforms for the animals to exit the water when needed.

When designing a naturalistic environment, always keep in mind your pet's specific needs. Some reptiles and amphibians are arboreal (tree-dwelling), while others are terrestrial or aquatic, so the habitat should reflect those behaviors.

## SUBSTRATES, DECORATIONS, AND HIDING SPOTS

The substrate is the material that covers the bottom of the enclosure and is an essential element of the habitat. The right substrate promotes healthy digestion, aids in humidity control, and allows for natural behaviors.

• Substrates for Reptiles: For land-dwelling reptiles, options like sand, coconut fiber, or cypress mulch can work well, depending on the species. Some reptiles, like geckos, benefit from loose substrates for burrowing, while others, like bearded dragons, do better on solid substrates such as tile or reptile carpet to prevent impaction from ingesting the substrate.

• Substrates for Amphibians: Amphibians typically require a more moisture-retentive substrate, such as sphagnum moss, coconut husk, or peat. These substrates help maintain the humidity levels needed for amphibians' skin respiration. Be sure to avoid substrates that may contain harmful chemicals like cedar or pine shavings.

• Decorations and Hiding Spots: Providing hiding spots is crucial for the mental and physical well-being of reptiles and amphibians. Hiding spots can help reduce stress, prevent territorial aggression, and give your pets a place to rest. Use natural elements like rocks, driftwood, or logs, or commercial hides that mimic the shapes of caves or burrows. Plants—either live or artificial—are a great addition to any enclosure, as they create more vertical space, help maintain humidity, and give your pets a place to explore. Live plants like ferns, ivy, and pothos are perfect for amphibians, while succulents or cacti are more suited to arid reptiles.

• Climbing and Basking Areas: For arboreal species, add climbing branches, vines, or shelves to mimic their natural environment. Basking platforms, rocks, or heat lamps should be provided for reptiles that require sunlight or heat to regulate their body temperature. Setting up the perfect habitat for reptiles and amphibians requires careful planning and understanding of the specific needs of each species. By choosing the right enclosure, maintaining proper lighting, heating, and humidity, and creating a naturalistic environment with suitable substrates and hiding spots, you can provide a thriving and enriching home for your cold-blooded pets. A well-designed habitat not only promotes your pet's health and well-being but also helps them exhibit natural behaviors, ensuring a happy and healthy life in captivity.

# CHAPTER TWO

# FEEDING AND NUTRITION FOR REPTILES AND AMPHIBIANS

Proper nutrition is vital for the health and well-being of reptiles and amphibians. Their dietary needs vary widely depending on their species, natural habitat, and specific physiological requirements. Whether you're feeding a carnivorous snake, an herbivorous tortoise, or an omnivorous frog, understanding the basics of reptile and amphibian nutrition is key to ensuring they thrive.

## GENERAL DIET GUIDELINES FOR REPTILES AND AMPHIBIANS

Reptiles and amphibians have highly specialized diets based on their natural behaviors and evolutionary needs. Their nutritional requirements include protein, fats, carbohydrates, fiber, vitamins, and minerals, all of which contribute to maintaining energy, bone health, and proper body function. However, there are some general guidelines that can help pet owners meet their pets' needs.

• Protein: Reptiles and amphibians that are carnivorous or omnivorous need high-quality protein sources. This can include live or pre-killed insects, fish, or small vertebrates. For herbivores, protein may come from plant-based sources like leafy greens, but it is usually less concentrated than in carnivorous diets.

• Fiber: Fiber is essential for digestion, especially in herbivorous reptiles like tortoises and iguanas. Leafy vegetables, hay, and grasses provide the necessary fiber to aid digestion and promote gut health.

• Water: Proper hydration is essential for all reptiles and amphibians. While amphibians often absorb moisture through their skin, reptiles drink water from bowls or absorb it through their food. Ensure that fresh, clean water is available at all times.

• Fresh vs. Frozen: Fresh food is often the best option for ensuring that your pet receives the most nutrients. However, frozen foods (like frozen insects, rodents, or fish) can also be used if fresh options aren't available, though these should be properly thawed before feeding.

## LIVE VS PREPARED FOODS WHAT'S BEST

One of the most common questions pet owners have is whether live or prepared foods are the best option for their reptiles and amphibians. Both have pros and cons, depending on the species and specific circumstances.

• Live Foods: Many reptiles and amphibians, especially carnivorous species, benefit from the natural hunting behavior that live food encourages. Live prey, such as crickets, worms, or small rodents, provides enrichment and stimulation, helping to mimic the wild hunting experience. Live food also tends to have higher nutritional value, particularly in terms of moisture content and movement, which can stimulate the pet's appetite and encourage natural feeding behaviors.

Pros: Higher nutritional value, promotes natural hunting behavior, encourages exercise.

Cons: Live food can be hard to store, may carry parasites or diseases, and may require frequent replenishment.

• Prepared Foods: Prepared foods, such as freeze-dried, canned, or pre-packaged meals, are convenient and often easier to store than live foods. They can be nutritionally balanced to meet the needs of specific species, ensuring that your pet receives the right amount of vitamins and minerals. However, some pets may be reluctant to accept these foods, and they may not provide the same enrichment as live food.

Pros: Convenient, easy to store, often nutritionally balanced.

Cons: May lack the stimulation of live food, some species may refuse them.

For most reptiles and amphibians, a combination of live food and prepared meals can offer the best of both worlds—providing nutrition and variety while allowing for enrichment and convenience.

# FEEDING SPECIFIC SPECIES SNAKES, LIZARDS, FROGS

Each species has unique dietary requirements. Here's a brief overview of the feeding needs of common reptiles and amphibians:

• Snakes: Snakes are obligate carnivores and eat a diet consisting primarily of mammals, birds, or reptiles. Depending on the snake species, food options might include mice, rats, chicks, or even larger prey like rabbits. They typically eat once every 5 to 10 days, depending on their size and metabolism. Pre-killed food is often safer for captive snakes to avoid the risk of injury.

• Lizards: Most lizards are either insectivores, herbivores, or omnivores. For insectivorous lizards, such as geckos or anoles, a diet of crickets, mealworms, or other insects is essential. Herbivorous species like iguanas and tortoises require a variety of leafy greens, vegetables, and some fruits. Omnivorous species, such as bearded dragons, need a mix of both animal-based and plant-based foods.

• Frogs: Most frogs are carnivorous, feeding on insects, small fish, and worms. Some amphibians, like tree frogs, may also consume small invertebrates like snails. While some species may accept pellets or freeze-dried foods, live prey such as crickets, fruit flies, and waxworms are preferred to ensure the frogs receive proper nutrition.

• Turtles and Tortoises: Tortoises are mostly herbivorous, requiring a diet high in fiber and calcium, consisting of grasses, leaves, and some fruits. Aquatic turtles are omnivores, eating a combination of fish, insects, vegetables, and commercial turtle pellets. Some turtles, like box turtles, may also enjoy small amounts of fruit or meat.

• Amphibians like Salamanders and Newts: These creatures are typically carnivorous, feeding on small insects, worms, and other invertebrates. They may also eat tiny crustaceans and mollusks if available. Always research the specific dietary requirements of your species to provide the best nutrition. Tailor their diet to suit their natural food sources, whether that's live prey, vegetation, or a mixture of both.

# SUPPLEMENTS AND VITAMINS FOR A BALANCED DIET

To ensure that your reptile or amphibian receives all the essential nutrients, supplements may be necessary. These include vitamins, minerals, and other nutrients that might be lacking in their diet, especially in captivity.

• Calcium: Many reptiles, particularly those with hard-shelled eggs or bones, need additional calcium to maintain healthy bones and prevent metabolic bone disease. Calcium powder can be sprinkled over their food, or calcium supplements can be added to their water. Tortoises, iguanas, and bearded dragons, for example, are particularly prone to calcium deficiencies.

• Vitamin D3: Vitamin D3 is crucial for the proper absorption of calcium. Without adequate D3, your pet may struggle to process calcium, leading to skeletal issues. Many reptiles and amphibians get Vitamin D3 through exposure to UVB light, but it can also be supplemented in their diet, especially if they are not getting enough natural sunlight.

• Multivitamins: To fill in any gaps in nutrition, a multivitamin supplement can be given periodically. These can help provide essential vitamins like Vitamin A, which is important for skin health and immune function.

• Phosphorus: Some reptiles and amphibians, particularly herbivores, need to maintain the right balance of calcium and phosphorus. Too much phosphorus can block calcium absorption, leading to deficiencies. Feeding reptiles and amphibians requires an understanding of their unique nutritional needs. Providing a diet that mimics their natural food sources, whether it's live food, prepared meals, or a mixture of both, will help ensure your pet stays healthy and active. Additionally, supplements like calcium, Vitamin D3, and multivitamins can help fill any dietary gaps and prevent deficiencies. By properly meeting their nutritional needs, you can help your cold-blooded companions live long, healthy lives in captivity.

## HEALTH AND CARE FOR YOUR REPTILES AND AMPHIBIANS

Reptiles and amphibians require specific care and attention to maintain their health and well-being in captivity. Understanding the signs of a healthy pet, knowing how to prevent common health issues, and being able to spot illness early are all essential for providing proper care. Additionally, proper handling and stress management can help reduce the risk of injury and improve the overall quality of life for your pet.

## SIGNS OF A HEALTHY PET

A healthy reptile or amphibian is active, alert, and free from visible signs of illness. While individual species may have some differences in appearance and behavior, there are general signs you can look for to gauge the health of your pet.

• Clear Eyes: Healthy reptiles and amphibians should have clear, bright eyes with no discharge or swelling. Cloudy or swollen eyes may indicate an infection or other health issue.

• Active and Alert Behavior: A healthy pet will be active during its typical active period, moving around its enclosure and showing interest in its surroundings. Lethargy or unresponsiveness can be a sign of stress or illness.

• Healthy Skin and Shedding: The skin should appear smooth and free of lesions, sores, or abrasions. For species that shed their skin (like snakes and some lizards), the shedding process should be gradual and complete. Stuck shed or incomplete shedding may indicate poor humidity levels or health issues.

• Normal Appetite: A healthy pet will show an interest in food, whether it's live prey, vegetables, or prepared meals. A lack of appetite may be an early warning sign of illness or stress.

• Proper Waste Elimination: Regular, healthy droppings are another indicator of your pet's health. Loose stools, excessive urination, or difficulty defecating can point to digestive issues or other health problems.

# COMMON HEALTH ISSUES AND HOW TO PREVENT THEM

There are several common health issues that affect reptiles and amphibians, many of which can be prevented through proper husbandry and care. Some of these issues include:

1. Metabolic Bone Disease (MBD):

Cause: Often caused by calcium and Vitamin D3 deficiencies, particularly in reptiles that don't receive enough UVB light.

Prevention: Provide UVB lighting to help your pet synthesize Vitamin D3 and ensure a proper calcium-rich diet. You can also supplement with calcium powder as needed.

2. Respiratory Infections:

Cause: Poor ventilation, improper humidity levels, or low temperatures can cause respiratory infections in reptiles and amphibians.

Prevention: Maintain proper humidity and temperature levels in the enclosure and ensure good ventilation. If your pet shows signs of labored breathing, mucus around the nose, or a swollen throat, consult a vet.

3. Parasites:

Cause: Internal and external parasites, such as worms, mites, and ticks, are common in reptiles and amphibians. Parasites can cause a range of symptoms, including weight loss, lethargy, and skin irritation.

Prevention: Quarantine new pets before introducing them to your collection, and provide routine parasite checks and deworming. Also, keep the enclosure clean and monitor your pet for unusual behavior.

4. Skin Infections:

Cause: Skin infections can result from bacterial or fungal exposure, poor enclosure conditions, or injuries.

Prevention: Maintain a clean, dry enclosure and handle your pet gently to avoid injury. Ensure proper humidity levels and avoid overcrowding.

5. Obesity:

Cause: Overfeeding, particularly with high-fat or high-protein foods, can lead to obesity, which affects a pet's mobility and overall health.

Prevention: Stick to a balanced, species-appropriate diet and avoid overfeeding. Monitor your pet's weight regularly and ensure they have space to exercise.

6. Dehydration:

Cause: Inadequate access to fresh water or poor humidity levels can lead to dehydration.

Prevention: Always provide fresh, clean water, and ensure proper humidity levels for your species. Amphibians often require more moisture than reptiles, so make sure their environment is sufficiently humid.

## SPOTTING ILLNESS EARLY SYMPTOMS AND TREATMENTS

Early detection of illness in reptiles and amphibians is crucial for successful treatment. Look out for the following symptoms, which may indicate that something is wrong:

• Changes in Behavior: Lethargy, loss of appetite, or unusual aggression can all be signs of illness or stress.

• Swollen Eyes or Skin: Swelling, redness, or discharge from the eyes or skin can be a sign of infection.

• Abnormal Bowel Movements: Diarrhea, constipation, or changes in the frequency or consistency of feces may indicate digestive issues.

• Respiratory Issues: Labored breathing, wheezing, or bubbling from the nose or mouth can point to a respiratory infection.

• Limping or Difficulty Moving: If your pet seems unable to move its limbs properly or is dragging its body, it could indicate a physical injury or neurological issue. If you notice any of these symptoms, consult a veterinarian experienced with reptiles and amphibians. They may need to perform tests, such as fecal exams, blood tests, or X-rays, to diagnose the problem. Early intervention is key to successful treatment.

## PROPER HANDLING AND STRESS MANAGEMENT

Handling reptiles and amphibians correctly is crucial for their physical and mental well-being.

Improper handling can lead to stress, injury, or even death in extreme cases.

• Handle with Care: Always handle your pet gently and with respect. Avoid grabbing or squeezing them tightly, as this can cause injury or stress. Many reptiles and amphibians are easily stressed, so it's essential to move slowly and calmly when interacting with them.

• Limit Handling: Reptiles and amphibians generally do not enjoy being handled frequently, especially species that are more solitary or territorial. Limit handling to short sessions, especially in the beginning, to avoid overwhelming your pet. Always allow your pet to acclimate to their environment before introducing handling.

• Stress Signs: Watch for signs of stress in your pet, such as rapid breathing, hiding, excessive scratching, or defensive postures. Stress can lead to weakened immune systems, making them more susceptible to illness. If your pet shows signs of stress, assess the environment (lighting, humidity, temperature) and handling techniques. If the stress persists, consider consulting an expert.

• Environmental Stress: Ensure your pet's enclosure is free from loud noises, excessive handling, or disturbances, which can cause unnecessary stress. Reptiles and amphibians are sensitive to changes in their environment, and sudden temperature shifts or changes in lighting can also contribute to stress. Caring for reptiles and amphibians requires attention to detail and an understanding of their unique health needs. Recognizing the signs of a healthy pet and knowing how to spot illness early can help ensure your pet lives a long, healthy life. Preventing common health issues through proper nutrition, hygiene, and habitat setup is essential, as is minimizing stress through appropriate handling and environmental conditions. Regular veterinary check-ups and prompt treatment for illness are crucial steps in providing the best care possible for your cold-blooded companions.

# CHAPTER THREE

# BREEDING REPTILES AND AMPHIBIANS

Breeding reptiles and amphibians in captivity is an exciting and rewarding endeavor, but it requires a deep understanding of their reproductive behaviors, habitat needs, and care for the young. Whether you're breeding for conservation, personal enjoyment, or education, providing the right conditions and ensuring the health of both the adults and their offspring is essential. Here's a guide to the basics of breeding these fascinating creatures, from courtship to raising young.

## THE BASICS OF BREEDING COURTSHIP AND REPRODUCTION

Breeding reptiles and amphibians typically follows a seasonal cycle, with many species requiring specific environmental cues to trigger reproduction. Understanding these cues and behaviors is crucial for successful breeding.

• Courtship and Mating:

In reptiles, courtship behaviors can vary widely by species. Some may involve visual displays like bright colors or head bobbing (common in many lizards), while others may use scent-marking or physical gestures like tail waving or biting (seen in snakes and certain frogs). Amphibians, particularly frogs, often rely on vocal calls to attract mates, with males calling from ponds or other water sources to draw females near.

Successful mating usually requires males and females to be kept in close proximity, and sometimes in a breeding-specific environment that mimics their natural conditions.

- Reproduction:

Most reptiles and amphibians are oviparous (egg-laying), although some reptiles (like certain species of snakes and lizards) are viviparous (live-bearing). The reproductive process typically involves internal fertilization, with males transferring sperm to females during copulation.

In amphibians, fertilization often occurs externally, especially in frogs and salamanders, where the female lays eggs in water and the male releases sperm over them.

## SETTING UP A BREEDING ENCLOSURE

Creating the right environment for breeding is key to successful reproduction. The breeding enclosure should cater to the species' specific needs, including temperature, humidity, space, and security.

• Size and Security: The enclosure should be large enough for both the male and female to move around comfortably and interact with each other. It should also be secure to prevent escape and protect the animals from predators. The space should allow for natural behaviors, such as hiding, climbing, or basking, depending on the species.

• Temperature and Humidity: Many reptiles and amphibians require specific temperature and humidity conditions to breed. For example, amphibians like frogs or salamanders may need cooler water temperatures or higher humidity during breeding seasons, while reptiles like certain species of lizards may require a temperature gradient in their enclosures to mimic seasonal changes.

• Habitat Features: Create an environment that encourages natural breeding behaviors. For amphibians, a water feature (such as a shallow pond or moist area) is essential for species that lay eggs in water. Reptiles may require specific hiding spots, basking areas, or even climbing structures to simulate natural habitats.

• Lighting: Many reptiles rely on UVB lighting to breed successfully, especially for egg-laying species. Some species may require exposure to specific light cycles (e.g., increased daylight during breeding seasons), while others may need a period of darkness to simulate winter conditions, triggering reproduction.

## EGG CARE INCUBATION AND HATCHING

Once mating has occurred and eggs are laid, proper egg care is crucial to ensuring successful hatching. Different species have distinct needs when it comes to incubation.

• Incubation Conditions:

The temperature and humidity levels for incubating reptile and amphibian eggs vary depending on the species. For reptiles, eggs typically need a warm, stable environment, with temperatures ranging from 75°F to 85°F (24°C to 29°C) for many species. Amphibians, such as frogs and salamanders, often require cooler or more humid conditions for their eggs to hatch.

For most reptiles, it is essential to maintain consistent temperatures to ensure the development of the embryos. Fluctuations can result in deformities or the failure of eggs to hatch.

• Incubation Medium:

Many breeders use an incubation medium, such as vermiculite, perlite, or moist sand, to maintain the right moisture level for the eggs. The medium should be kept moist but not soaking wet. Proper ventilation in the incubator is also critical to prevent mold or fungal growth.

• Incubation Time:

Depending on the species, the incubation period can vary significantly. For example, turtle eggs may take 60 to 90 days to hatch, while geckos can take 30 to 60 days. Some species, particularly amphibians, may have shorter or longer incubation periods depending on environmental conditions and egg size.

## RAISING THE YOUNG FROM HATCHLING TO ADULT

Once the eggs hatch, it's important to provide the right care for the young reptiles or amphibians. The care requirements for hatchlings can differ significantly from adults.

• Initial Care: Hatchlings may be fragile and require a calm, low-stress environment. Young reptiles and amphibians typically need to be separated from the adults, especially if the species is known for being territorial or predatory.

• Feeding: Hatchlings may have different dietary needs compared to adults. Many species of reptiles and amphibians require live food, such as insects, worms, or small prey. Some species might also eat small plant material. It's essential to provide appropriately sized food and offer a balanced diet to promote healthy growth.

• Humidity and Temperature: Newly hatched reptiles and amphibians may require different humidity and temperature levels than adults. Some species may be more sensitive during their early stages of life, and it is important to create a controlled environment that supports their growth.

• Monitoring Growth: Keep an eye on the development of the young, including their size, behavior, and overall health. Some species may go through distinct life stages that require different care, such as amphibians transitioning from aquatic larvae to terrestrial adults.

• Releasing or Keeping the Young: Depending on your goals, you may choose to keep the young reptiles or amphibians as pets or breed them in the future. Alternatively, if breeding is done for conservation purposes, the young may be released into appropriate habitats. Breeding reptiles and amphibians requires careful planning, knowledge, and dedication. Understanding courtship behaviors, setting up a proper breeding enclosure, providing the right incubation conditions, and caring for the young are all vital components of the breeding process. Whether you are breeding for hobby, education, or conservation, ensuring the health and safety of the adults and their offspring should always be your top priority. With the right approach, breeding reptiles and amphibians can be a fulfilling and successful experience.

## HANDLING AND INTERACTION WITH REPTILES AND AMPHIBIANS

While reptiles and amphibians may not be as overtly affectionate as dogs or cats, they can form strong bonds with their owners and respond to handling when done correctly. Learning how to interact safely with these creatures, understanding their body language, and establishing trust can lead to a more positive experience for both pet and owner. Here's a guide to handling and interacting with your reptiles and amphibians.

## SAFE HANDLING TECHNIQUES

Handling reptiles and amphibians properly is essential for both their well-being and yours.

These creatures are often more delicate than other pets and require specific techniques to avoid stress or injury.

• Start Slowly: When first introducing yourself to a new reptile or amphibian, take it slow. Let your pet become accustomed to your presence before attempting any physical interaction. Many species need time to feel safe and secure in their environment.

• Support Their Body Properly: Always support your reptile or amphibian properly when picking them up. For lizards, place one hand under the chest and another under the hind legs to provide full support. Snakes should be picked up gently and supported along their bodies. Amphibians like frogs or salamanders should be held carefully with one hand under their belly, ensuring their legs and body are supported.

• Avoid Grabbing by the Tail or Limbs: Some reptiles and amphibians may lose their tails as a defense mechanism (e.g., some species of lizards). Avoid grabbing them by the tail, and never pull on their limbs. Handle them gently to prevent stress and potential harm.

• Minimal Handling for Sensitive Species: Not all reptiles and amphibians enjoy being handled. Species like turtles, snakes, or certain amphibians may become stressed with too much interaction. It's important to respect their comfort level and not force handling.

• Wash Your Hands Before and After Handling: Always wash your hands thoroughly before and after handling your reptile or amphibian. Reptiles and amphibians can carry bacteria (such as Salmonella) that can be transmitted to humans, so hygiene is crucial.

# UNDERSTANDING ANIMAL BEHAVIOR AND BODY LANGUAGE

Reptiles and amphibians communicate through body language, and understanding these signals can help you interpret their mood and ensure you're providing proper care.

• Signs of Stress: Stress in reptiles and amphibians can manifest through behaviors such as hiding, excessive movement, aggression, or a refusal to eat. If your pet seems restless or shows signs of aggression when handled, it may be stressed or scared. Avoid handling them during this time.

• Signs of Comfort: A relaxed and comfortable pet will often have a calm, still posture. Reptiles and amphibians may also exhibit slow, deliberate movements when they are content. Snakes, for example, may coil up in a relaxed position or gently explore their environment when they feel secure.

• Defensive Behavior: When feeling threatened, many reptiles and amphibians will display defensive behaviors such as puffing up their bodies, hissing, or making themselves look larger. Amphibians, like some frogs, may secrete toxins as a form of defense. It's important not to take these behaviors personally; they are natural instincts.

• Signs of Affection or Interest: While reptiles and amphibians may not show affection in the way mammals do, many can form bonds with their owners. Some species of lizards, such as bearded dragons, may display interest by approaching their owners or allowing themselves to be handled more willingly. Snakes may become more relaxed with gentle handling over time and may even crawl toward their owner's hand.

• Tail Waving or Flicking: In certain species, tail movements can signal various things. For example, lizards may use tail flicks or waves to communicate with other animals or humans. Pay attention to these subtle cues to understand their mood.

# BUILDING TRUST WITH YOUR PET

Trust is a key element of any positive relationship with your reptile or amphibian. It takes time, patience, and consistency to build trust with these pets, but the effort is well worth it.

• Consistent Routine: Reptiles and amphibians thrive on routine. Providing consistent feeding schedules, environmental conditions, and handling practices can help them feel more secure and reduce anxiety. Over time, they will learn to associate you with positive experiences.

• Gentle Interaction: Always handle your pet gently and calmly, using a soft and slow approach. Avoid sudden movements or loud noises around them, as they can be easily startled. Allow your pet time to explore your hands or the environment at their own pace.

• Positive Reinforcement: Some reptiles and amphibians can learn to associate certain actions with rewards. For instance, feeding your pet by hand or offering treats after interaction can encourage positive associations with you.

• Respect Their Space: Reptiles and amphibians may need time alone, especially after being handled. Always allow them to retreat to a safe, quiet place where they can rest and feel secure. Don't force interaction, and respect their need for space.

• Avoid Overhandling: Too much handling can lead to stress and even health problems for your pet. Limit handling to short periods, especially for species that are not as tolerant of human interaction.

# SOCIALIZATION AND BONDING TIPS FOR REPTILES AND AMPHIBIANS

While reptiles and amphibians may not form social bonds in the same way that mammals do, many can develop familiarity and comfort with their owners.

• Start from Young Age: The earlier you begin handling and interacting with your pet, the more likely they are to become accustomed to your presence. For species that tolerate handling, this early exposure can help create a more trusting and social relationship.

• Observing and Interacting During Feeding: You can interact with your pet while feeding, which can help build positive associations. Offer food by hand when appropriate, and try to engage them without overwhelming them. Watching your pet hunt or feed can also provide insights into their behavior.

• Respect Their Natural Instincts: Some reptiles and amphibians are solitary by nature and may not seek social interaction, even with other animals of their species. In these cases, simply allowing them to be in a controlled environment where they feel safe is the best way to bond.

• Behavioral Training: Although reptiles and amphibians don't typically respond to training like dogs, some species can be conditioned to perform basic actions, such as eating from your hand or responding to gentle touch. With patience, you can teach them to tolerate certain behaviors, like entering and exiting their enclosure or sitting on your lap. Handling and interacting with reptiles and amphibians require patience, respect, and an understanding of their unique needs and behaviors. By using safe handling techniques, observing their body language, and taking the time to build trust, you can form a meaningful bond with these fascinating pets. Remember that not all reptiles and amphibians are social animals, so it's important to respect their comfort level and create an environment that promotes their health and happiness. With the right approach, your relationship with your reptile or amphibian can be both rewarding and fulfilling.

# CHAPTER FOUR

## COMMON SPECIES OF REPTILES AND AMPHIBIANS

Whether you're a seasoned pet owner or a first-timer, understanding the different species of reptiles and amphibians can help you make informed decisions about which one is right for you. From commonly kept reptiles like snakes and lizards to the fascinating world of amphibians like frogs and salamanders, each species comes with its own set of unique characteristics, behaviors, and care needs. Below is an overview of the most popular reptiles and amphibians, along with a look at some exotic species and their specific care requirements.

# POPULAR REPTILES SNAKES, LIZARDS, TURTLES, AND MORE

Snakes

Snakes are one of the most common reptiles kept as pets. Known for their fascinating behavior and varied appearances, they come in many species and sizes. Here are a few popular pet snakes:

• Corn Snake: This non-venomous, docile snake is known for its vibrant colors and patterns. Corn snakes are easy to care for and can live for 15-20 years, making them a popular choice for beginners.

• Ball Python: Ball pythons are gentle and shy snakes, often seeking comfort in dark, secure spaces. They are easy to care for and have a slow-growing, manageable size.

• King Snake: These snakes are hardy and easy to handle, often kept for their diverse color patterns and docile nature.

• Boa Constrictor: While a bit larger and requiring more space, boas make great pets for more experienced snake owners due to their calm demeanor and slow movements.

Lizards

Lizards are another popular category of reptiles, ranging from tiny geckos to large monitor lizards. Some well-known pet lizards include:

• Bearded Dragon: These friendly and social lizards are known for their calm temperament and distinctive "beard." Bearded dragons are easy to care for, requiring a warm, dry environment and a balanced diet of insects and vegetables.

• Leopard Gecko: Known for their striking patterns and manageable size, leopard geckos are nocturnal lizards that require minimal care. They are perfect for beginners.

• Iguanas: Larger species like the green iguana are often kept by more experienced reptile enthusiasts. Iguanas are herbivores and need a large habitat to thrive.

• Blue-Tongue Skink: These lizards are known for their striking blue tongue and docile nature. They are omnivorous and require a balanced diet, along with a warm environment.

Turtles

Turtles are unique among reptiles due to their hard shells and aquatic or semi-aquatic lifestyles. Common pet turtles include:

• Red-Eared Slider: This aquatic turtle is one of the most commonly kept turtles. Red-eared sliders are known for their adaptability and ability to live in various aquatic environments.

• Box Turtle: A land-dwelling turtle species that thrives in warm, humid environments. They can live for many years and require a secure enclosure with ample space.

• Russian Tortoise: A land turtle species known for its small size and docile behavior, making it a great choice for beginners.

Other Reptiles

There are many other types of reptiles that may appeal to enthusiasts, including:

• Chameleons: Known for their ability to change color and unique personalities, chameleons are visually stunning pets that require specific care for humidity and temperature.

• Monitor Lizards: Larger and more complex to care for, monitor lizards need a spacious enclosure and a varied diet. They are suited for more experienced reptile keepers.

# AMPHIBIANS FROGS, SALAMANDERS, NEWTS, AND CAECILIANS

Amphibians are often fascinating creatures, living both in water and on land throughout their life stages. They are well-known for their vibrant colors and unique behaviors. Here are some of the most popular amphibians:

Frogs

Frogs are often the first amphibians people think of, and many species make great pets.

• African Dwarf Frog: A small, aquatic frog that thrives in freshwater tanks. They're easy to care for and great for beginners.

• American Green Tree Frog: Known for their vivid green color and small size, these frogs are low-maintenance and can live comfortably in a humid tank.

• Pacman Frog: A larger, more exotic frog known for its round shape and large mouth. Pacman frogs are relatively easy to care for but require a diet of live prey and specific humidity levels.

• White's Tree Frog: This species is known for its calm demeanor and ability to adapt to different environments. They are excellent for beginners.

Salamanders

Salamanders are another fascinating group of amphibians, often kept for their colorful appearances and aquatic nature.

• Eastern Newt: This small, semi-aquatic amphibian is known for its bright orange color and is commonly kept in aquatic setups.

• Axolotl: A unique type of salamander that retains its larval form throughout its life, known for its regenerative abilities and ability to grow back lost limbs. Axolotls are kept in freshwater aquariums and require cool water temperatures.

Newts

Newts are closely related to salamanders and often kept in similar conditions.

• Chinese Fire-Bellied Newt: Known for its striking red-orange belly, this newt thrives in both land and aquatic environments.

• Japanese Fire-Bellied Newt: Like its Chinese counterpart, the Japanese fire-bellied newt is a vibrant amphibian that is relatively easy to care for.

Caecilians

Caecilians are lesser-known amphibians that are often overlooked as pets, though they can be interesting for experienced amphibian keepers.

• Caecilian Species: These legless amphibians are more elusive and can be challenging to care for, as they require a very specific, moist environment.

# EXOTIC AND RARE SPECIES WHAT TO KNOW BEFORE YOU KEEP THEM

Exotic and rare reptiles and amphibians can be alluring, but they often come with increased care challenges. Here are a few things to keep in mind before keeping an exotic species:

• Research Thoroughly: Exotic species often have very specific environmental needs, such as particular temperatures, humidity levels, or dietary requirements. Ensure that you fully understand the care needs of the species you're interested in.

• Availability and Legal Concerns: Some rare species may be endangered or regulated by local or national laws. Always check local regulations before purchasing a rare species to ensure you're not violating any laws.

• Increased Cost: Exotic species can be more expensive to purchase and maintain. They may require specialized enclosures, food, and medical care that can drive up the overall cost of ownership.

• Breeding and Conservation: Some exotic species may only thrive in captivity if bred in controlled environments. Consider supporting breeders who focus on conservation efforts.

# IDENTIFYING CHARACTERISTICS AND UNIQUE CARE REQUIREMENTS

Each reptile and amphibian species comes with unique characteristics and care needs. Here's a brief overview of identifying features and special requirements:

• Skin and Shedding: Reptiles like snakes and lizards often shed their skin as they grow.

Amphibians, on the other hand, have permeable skin that can absorb water and nutrients. It's important to keep their environments moist enough for proper skin function.

• Diet: While many reptiles are carnivorous (e.g., snakes and certain lizards), others are herbivores (e.g., iguanas and tortoises). Amphibians like frogs are usually insectivores, while others like the axolotl can be both carnivorous and omnivorous. Always cater to their dietary needs by providing the correct live or prepared foods.

• Enclosure Setup: Enclosures vary significantly from species to species. Aquatic species, like many frogs and turtles, require water setups, while others, like desert reptiles, need dry, hot environments. The enclosure should always mimic their natural habitat to ensure they thrive. Whether you're drawn to the beauty of snakes, the quirky personalities of lizards, or the fascinating world of amphibians, keeping reptiles and amphibians as pets can be a rewarding experience. By understanding the needs of popular species, as well as the challenges posed by exotic and rare species, you can create the perfect environment for your new pet and enjoy their unique charm and behavior for years to come.

## CONSERVATION AND ETHICAL CONSIDERATIONS

Reptiles and amphibians are vital components of our ecosystems, and their conservation is crucial for maintaining biodiversity. However, the popularity of keeping these creatures as pets has led to several conservation and ethical concerns. This section explores the importance of conservation for reptiles and amphibians, the legal and ethical aspects of keeping exotic pets, and how pet owners can support wildlife preservation efforts.

# THE IMPORTANCE OF CONSERVATION FOR REPTILES AND AMPHIBIANS

Reptiles and amphibians play essential roles in ecosystems as predators, prey, and pollinators. They help regulate insect populations, decompose organic matter, and maintain the balance of their habitats. Unfortunately, many species of reptiles and amphibians are facing significant threats to their survival, such as:

• Habitat Destruction: Urbanization, deforestation, and agricultural expansion are destroying the natural habitats of reptiles and amphibians, making it difficult for them to survive and reproduce in the wild.

• Climate Change: Changes in temperature, rainfall, and the availability of water sources are impacting the delicate balance that reptiles and amphibians need to thrive. Species that rely on specific climates or seasonal patterns may struggle to adapt.

• Pollution: Pollution, particularly chemical pollutants in water sources, is a growing concern for amphibians, whose permeable skin makes them especially vulnerable to toxins.

• Over-Exploitation: The collection of reptiles and amphibians for the pet trade, as well as for medicinal or cultural purposes, can lead to population declines. Many species are caught from the wild and sold without regard for their well-being or sustainability.

Conservation efforts, both in-situ (in the wild) and ex-situ (in captivity), are essential to ensure that these species do not face extinction. Support for local and global initiatives that protect their habitats, as well as programs that breed and release endangered species, is vital to the long-term survival of many reptiles and amphibians.

# LEGAL AND ETHICAL ASPECTS OF KEEPING EXOTIC PETS

The exotic pet trade has come under increasing scrutiny due to ethical concerns, particularly regarding the welfare of animals taken from their natural habitats. There are several important legal and ethical aspects to consider before owning a reptile or amphibian:

Legal Considerations

• Permits and Regulations: Many countries and states have strict regulations governing the ownership of exotic pets. It's important to check the legal status of the species you're interested in before acquiring it. In some areas, certain species are protected by law, and keeping them as pets may require special permits.

• CITES (Convention on International Trade in Endangered Species): This international agreement aims to ensure that the trade in wild animals and plants does not threaten their survival. Reptiles and amphibians listed under CITES require special permits for international trade. If you're considering purchasing an exotic species, ensure it's legally sourced and not a species at risk of extinction.

Ethical Considerations

• Wild-Caught vs. Captive-Bred: The ethics of purchasing wild-caught reptiles and amphibians are a significant concern. Wild-caught animals often face stress, injury, and illness during capture and transport. Captive-bred reptiles and amphibians are generally a better option, as they help reduce the pressure on wild populations. Look for reputable breeders who follow ethical breeding practices.

• Animal Welfare: Ethical pet ownership means providing appropriate living conditions, care, and enrichment for your pet. Reptiles and amphibians often require specialized environments to thrive. Owners should be aware of the physical, psychological, and social needs of their pets and provide a habitat that meets their specific needs.

# HOW TO SUPPORT WILDLIFE PRESERVATION EFFORTS

As a responsible pet owner or enthusiast, you can play a crucial role in supporting the conservation of reptiles and amphibians. Here are some ways you can contribute to wildlife preservation efforts:

1. Support Conservation Organizations: Many organizations are dedicated to protecting reptiles and amphibians in the wild. These include groups like the International Union for Conservation of Nature (IUCN), Wildlife Conservation Society (WCS), and Save the Frogs, which work on research, habitat preservation, and species recovery efforts. Donations, fundraising, and

awareness campaigns are ways you can support these initiatives.

2. Promote Sustainable Practices: Opt for sustainably sourced pet reptiles and amphibians. This means buying only from breeders who engage in responsible breeding practices and who prioritize the well-being of animals. Avoid supporting the illegal pet trade, which often exploits animals and endangers their populations.

3. Educate Others: Spread awareness about the importance of reptile and amphibian conservation. Educating fellow pet owners, schools, and local communities about these creatures' ecological roles and conservation needs can help foster a culture of respect and protection for wildlife.

4. Contribute to Habitat Restoration Projects: Many organizations are involved in habitat restoration projects that help protect the natural

environments of reptiles and amphibians. Volunteering or donating to these initiatives can make a significant impact.

5. Participate in Citizen Science: Some organizations and research groups engage in citizen science, where everyday people can contribute to the study and conservation of reptiles and amphibians. Reporting sightings, participating in surveys, or tracking local populations can help scientists gather crucial data on species health.

## AVOIDING THE ILLEGAL PET TRADE

The illegal pet trade is a major contributor to the decline in reptile and amphibian populations. Many exotic species are taken from the wild and sold on the black market without regard for their long-term survival or the ethical implications.

Here's how you can help avoid the illegal pet trade:

• Buy From Reputable Sources: Only purchase reptiles and amphibians from licensed breeders, pet stores, or rescue organizations that adhere to ethical standards. Always ask about the source of the animals and whether they are captive-bred.

• Research the Species: Be cautious of species that are rare or have high market value. If a species seems too good to be true, it may be a sign that it has been illegally collected or is being traded without proper documentation.

• Report Suspicious Activities: If you suspect that an animal is being sold illegally, report it to local authorities or wildlife protection agencies. The more people who stand against the illegal pet trade, the less profit it will generate. The conservation and ethical considerations surrounding reptile and amphibian ownership are crucial for the protection of these fascinating species. By understanding the importance of conservation, adhering to legal guidelines, and supporting sustainable practices, pet owners can contribute to the preservation of reptiles and amphibians in the wild. Choosing to buy from ethical breeders, supporting wildlife preservation efforts, and avoiding the illegal pet trade are essential steps in ensuring that future generations can appreciate and care for these incredible creatures.

# CHAPTER FIVE

## TROUBLESHOOTING COMMON PROBLEMS

Even with the best care, pet reptiles and amphibians can sometimes face issues related to their behavior, health, or environment. Understanding how to troubleshoot common problems is essential for ensuring the well-being of your pets. This section explores common issues and provides guidance on how to handle them effectively.

## HANDLING BEHAVIORAL ISSUES: AGGRESSION, STRESS, AND MORE

Behavioral problems can arise in reptiles and amphibians due to a variety of factors such as stress, poor environmental conditions, or improper handling. Below are some common behavioral issues and how to address them:

Aggression

Aggression in reptiles and amphibians can be triggered by territoriality, mating behaviors, or stress. Common aggressive species include snakes, certain lizards, and turtles. Signs of aggression may include hissing, puffing up, biting, or defensive postures.

• Solution:

Ensure your pet's environment is spacious enough and that it is not feeling threatened by other animals or territorial disputes.

Avoid sudden movements or overstimulation when interacting with the animal.

Separate aggressive individuals, especially during breeding seasons, as this can exacerbate territorial behavior.

If handling, use calm, slow movements to avoid startling your pet.

Stress

Reptiles and amphibians are particularly sensitive to stress, which can lead to health issues such as poor eating habits, hiding, and lethargy. Stress may result from environmental changes, handling, or an unbalanced habitat.

• Solution:

Minimize handling to avoid overwhelming the animal.

Ensure proper lighting, temperature, and humidity in their environment to reduce stressors.

Avoid placing multiple pets in the same enclosure unless they are compatible.

Consider using natural hiding spots to allow your pet to retreat when it feels insecure.

Escape Attempts

Some reptiles, such as snakes and lizards, may attempt to escape from their enclosure. This can happen if they are not comfortable in their habitat or if the enclosure is not secure enough.

• Solution:

Check that the enclosure is escape-proof by ensuring that lids, doors, and screens are tightly sealed.

Ensure the habitat is large enough and that your pet has plenty of enrichment to occupy its time.

Address any environmental issues that may be causing discomfort, such as temperature extremes or lack of hiding spots.

# DEALING WITH FEEDING DIFFICULTIES

Feeding problems are common in reptiles and amphibians, especially when they are new to captivity or undergoing a molt, hibernation, or breeding season. Here are a few common feeding issues and how to solve them:

Refusal to Eat

A sudden lack of appetite can be worrying for pet owners. Various factors may contribute to a reptile or amphibian refusing food, including stress, improper diet, incorrect temperature, or illness.

• Solution:

Double-check the habitat conditions to ensure they are within the optimal range for the species. Adjust temperature, humidity, and lighting if needed.

Offer food that matches the species' natural preferences (live vs. pre-killed, insects vs. vegetables).

Offer smaller, easier-to-eat food items or try different food textures to see what appeals to your pet.

Ensure your pet is not stressed or overcrowded in its enclosure.

## OVERFEEDING OR UNDERFEEDING

Reptiles and amphibians can be overfed or underfed, which can lead to obesity or malnutrition. Overfeeding often leads to obesity in reptiles, while underfeeding can result in malnourishment.

• Solution:

Stick to a regular feeding schedule with portion control. Offer food appropriate to your pet's age, size, and species.

Monitor your pet's weight regularly, and adjust food portions accordingly.

Consult with a veterinarian if unsure about how much or how often to feed your pet.

## PROBLEMS WITH LIVE FOOD

Some species rely on live food, which can sometimes be difficult to obtain or present issues such as introducing parasites or diseases into the enclosure.

• Solution:

Ensure that live food is sourced from a reputable supplier to minimize the risk of introducing parasites.

Consider offering prey that has been gut-loaded (fed nutritious food before being offered to the pet) to improve nutritional value.

If live food is not ideal, consult with your veterinarian or reptile specialist for alternative dietary options.

## COMMON MISTAKES AND HOW TO AVOID THEM

Even experienced reptile and amphibian owners make occasional mistakes. Here are some common mistakes and how to avoid them:

## IMPROPER ENCLOSURE SETUP

One of the most common mistakes is not providing an environment that meets the specific needs of the pet. Each species has unique habitat requirements, such as the right temperature, humidity, substrate, and hiding spots.

• Solution:

Research the specific needs of the species you own before setting up its habitat.

Use appropriate heating and lighting sources to create a day-night cycle that matches the animal's natural environment.

Regularly clean and maintain the enclosure to prevent the buildup of harmful bacteria or mold.

## Over or Underhandling

Handling reptiles and amphibians too frequently or inappropriately can lead to stress, injury, or even death. Many reptiles do not enjoy being handled, and some amphibians are particularly sensitive to stress.

• Solution:

Handle your pets only when necessary and avoid overstimulating them.

Respect your pet's boundaries by allowing them to come to you or interact at their own pace.

Ensure that handling is done gently and with both hands for security, especially for species that are more fragile.

# NEGLECTING REGULAR HEALTH CHECKS

Failing to monitor your pet's health regularly can lead to undiagnosed illnesses or issues becoming more serious over time.

• Solution:

Regularly check your pet for signs of illness such as lethargy, abnormal skin shedding, discolored feces, or lack of appetite.

Schedule routine checkups with a reptile vet to ensure your pet is healthy and free from parasites or diseases.

# EMERGENCY CARE WHAT TO DO IN A CRISIS

Emergencies can happen unexpectedly. Whether it's an injury, illness, or environmental disaster, knowing how to respond quickly can make a significant difference in your pet's survival.

Signs of Distress

If your reptile or amphibian is showing signs of distress, including abnormal behavior, labored breathing, or disorientation, immediate action is necessary.

• Solution:

Remain calm and try to assess the situation carefully.

If possible, isolate your pet from other animals and place it in a safe, quiet space.

Contact a veterinarian who specializes in reptiles and amphibians as soon as possible for advice or emergency care.

**Handling Injuries**

Injuries such as broken limbs, bites, or burns can occur in reptiles and amphibians. It's important to act quickly to prevent further damage.

• Solution:

If the injury is severe, do not attempt to treat it yourself. Wrap your pet in a soft cloth or towel to reduce stress and transport it to a veterinarian immediately.

For minor injuries, gently clean the wound with saline solution, and keep the animal in a quiet, stress-free environment until you can consult with a vet.

# DEALING WITH TEMPERATURE EXTREMES

Reptiles and amphibians are highly sensitive to temperature changes, and exposure to extreme heat or cold can be life-threatening.

• Solution:

If your pet is exposed to temperatures outside its preferred range, immediately return it to the appropriate conditions.

If hypothermia is suspected, warm the animal slowly using a heat source (not directly), and seek veterinary care immediately.

For heat stress, move the animal to a cooler, shaded area and ensure it is hydrated.

By understanding these common problems and their solutions, you can better care for your reptile or amphibian, providing a healthy and fulfilling life for your pet.

# ADVANCED CARE AND SPECIAL CONSIDERATIONS

When it comes to keeping reptiles and amphibians as pets, the journey doesn't end with basic care. As an experienced pet owner, you'll encounter advanced challenges that require specialized knowledge and techniques. From caring for rare species to ensuring your pet's mental health, this section dives deeper into the complexities of advanced care and considerations, helping you provide the best possible environment for your exotic companion.

## ADVANCED SPECIES CARE FOR UNIQUE AND RARE PETS

Caring for rare or exotic species comes with a set of challenges that differ from those associated with more common reptiles and amphibians. These animals often have more specific care requirements, making them suitable only for experienced hobbyists.

# UNIQUE AND RARE REPTILES AND AMPHIBIANS

Species such as the Indonesian Blue Tongue Skink, the Madagascar Leaf-Tailed Gecko, or the Amazon Milk Frog are not only fascinating but also require specialized environments, diets, and care routines.

• Solution:

Research: Extensive research is crucial before acquiring any rare species. Know their habitat, social behaviors, diet, and specific environmental needs.

Proper Enclosure: Ensure their enclosure replicates their natural habitat as closely as possible, including temperature, humidity, and substrate.

Feeding: Rare species may have particular dietary needs, such as specific insects or plants, and some might even require supplementation to avoid nutritional deficiencies.

Vet Care: Ensure that you have access to a reptile veterinarian who has experience with the species you're caring for, as they may be prone to specific health issues.

# ENVIRONMENTAL ENRICHMENT FOR YOUR PET'S MENTAL HEALTH

Reptiles and amphibians, like any pet, can benefit from environmental enrichment that stimulates their senses and natural behaviors. Mental stimulation is just as important as physical health, especially for intelligent and active species.

# WHAT IS ENVIRONMENTAL ENRICHMENT

Environmental enrichment involves making your pet's enclosure more engaging and stimulating. For reptiles and amphibians, this can include a variety of elements such as naturalistic settings, hiding spots, and interactive features that encourage exploration and problem-solving.

• Solution:

Variety in Substrate: Provide a mix of substrates that encourage digging, burrowing, or climbing, depending on the species. For example, sand, soil, and coconut fiber can offer different textures.

Climbing Structures: Use branches, rocks, and vines to create a vertical dimension for climbing reptiles like geckos and chameleons.

Water Features: Some amphibians, such as frogs, thrive in water-rich environments. Adding small ponds or misting systems can help maintain the natural habitat for these species.

Foraging Opportunities: Scatter food around the enclosure to encourage foraging behavior, mimicking the natural search for food. Live prey can also offer an enriching challenge for carnivorous reptiles.

Interactive Items: Introduce puzzle feeders or movable elements that require problem-solving, keeping your pet's mind active and engaged.

## CREATING A BIOACTIVE TERRARIUM

A bioactive terrarium is an enclosure that mimics the natural ecosystem, providing not only a home for your pet but also a sustainable environment that includes live plants, beneficial insects, and microorganisms.

What is a Bioactive Terrarium?

A bioactive terrarium is designed to function as a self-sustaining ecosystem, where plants, animals, and bacteria work together to break down waste and keep the environment clean. The inclusion of live plants and small cleanup crew insects (such as springtails and isopods) helps regulate humidity, temperature, and waste.

• Solution:

Live Plants: Select plants that thrive in the humidity and temperature conditions required by your pet. Plants such as ferns, mosses, and tropical species can create a lush, healthy environment.

Cleanup Crew: Springtails, isopods, and earthworms are often used to break down waste materials, keeping the terrarium clean without the need for frequent deep cleanings.

Proper Layers: Create a layered substrate with gravel at the bottom for drainage, followed by a layer of activated charcoal to prevent odors, and top with a nutrient-rich soil mix for plant growth.

Balance: Make sure the system is balanced by monitoring moisture levels, plant growth, and animal activity. A bioactive setup can help reduce the need for frequent cleaning, as it mimics the natural decomposition process.

## BREEDING CHALLENGES AND TIPS FOR EXPERTS

Breeding reptiles and amphibians is a rewarding but challenging aspect of advanced care. It requires a thorough understanding of the species' breeding habits, environmental conditions, and reproductive needs. Some species can be especially difficult to breed, and it's essential to know how to handle these challenges.

# COMMON BREEDING CHALLENGES

Breeding reptiles and amphibians may require specific temperature and humidity fluctuations, seasonal cycles, and correct environmental triggers. Some species also require a period of dormancy (brumation for reptiles, hibernation for amphibians) before they will breed.

• Solution:

Environmental Control: Adjust lighting, temperature, and humidity to simulate the conditions that trigger mating behavior in the wild. For example, some species breed after a "winter" period where temperatures are lowered.

Separation and Compatibility: Mating can sometimes lead to aggression. Make sure the male and female are compatible, and separate them if aggression occurs.

Encouraging Natural Behavior: For some species, you may need to create seasonal changes in their environment (like a dry period followed by a wet season) to encourage breeding.

Egg Incubation: Proper care of the eggs, including temperature and humidity control, is essential for successful hatching. Some species require specific temperature gradients, and others may require a cooling period.

## Raising the Young

Caring for hatchlings or tadpoles requires its own set of skills. Newborn reptiles and amphibians often need special conditions for growth, especially with respect to temperature, humidity, and feeding.

• Solution:

Separate Housing: Baby reptiles and amphibians often need their own enclosures, as they can be more sensitive to environmental fluctuations and aggressive adults.

Diet: Hatchlings or young amphibians may need smaller, more frequent feedings than adults. Live food such as small insects or worms may be required for carnivorous species.

Growth Monitoring: Keep an eye on the young for signs of malnutrition, stress, or illness, as they are more vulnerable than adults.

In conclusion, providing advanced care for reptiles and amphibians involves understanding not just their basic needs, but also their psychological well-being, breeding habits, and environmental complexities. Whether you're caring for rare species, designing a bioactive terrarium, or tackling breeding challenges, these specialized aspects of pet care ensure that your pets thrive in a well-maintained, enriched environment.

# FINAL THOUGHTS ON RESPONSIBLE PET OWNERSHIP

Being a responsible reptile and amphibian owner means prioritizing the well-being of your pets in every aspect of their care. From setting up the right environment to providing a balanced diet, handling them with respect, and ensuring their mental and physical health, each decision you make should reflect a commitment to their long-term health and happiness. Ethical pet ownership also means supporting conservation efforts, avoiding the illegal pet trade, and respecting wildlife by not removing animals from their natural habitats.

## LIFELONG CARE PREPARING FOR LONG-TERM COMMITMENT

Reptiles and amphibians often live for many years, some even decades, so keeping them as pets is a lifelong commitment. Species like turtles, snakes, and geckos can have lifespans ranging from 10 to 50 years, and some amphibians, like certain frogs, can live for 20 years or more. This long lifespan means that you need to be prepared for ongoing care, including maintaining their habitat, monitoring their health, and being ready for any changes in their needs over time.

Before acquiring a pet reptile or amphibian, consider the long-term responsibilities:

• Consistent Care: Be ready to provide continuous care and maintenance for their environment and well-being.

• Emergency Planning: Have a plan in place for emergencies, whether it's finding a qualified vet or arranging for care during vacations.

• End-of-Life Care: As with any pet, it's important to plan for your pet's aging process, including dealing with potential health decline and managing their final stages of life with compassion.

## Conclusion

Keeping reptiles and amphibians as pets can be an incredibly rewarding experience, offering a unique opportunity to connect with some of the most fascinating creatures on the planet. However, it's important to recognize that responsible pet ownership involves more than just providing food and shelter; it requires dedication, education, and a deep understanding of the needs of these animals.

In summary, reptile and amphibian care is an enriching and fulfilling hobby, but it requires a responsible, long-term commitment. Through continued education, ethical practices, and dedicated care, you can build a lasting, positive relationship with your cold-blooded companions, contributing to their well-being while enjoying the unique rewards they offer as pets.